S0-AGI-249

The Walking Dead Comic vs TV Show Differences Trivia Quiz Book

Copyright 2013,
All rights reserved.

Published by Mega Media Depot
P.O. Box 945
Prospect Heights, Il 60070

Manufactured in the United States of America

Some of the images in this book are used under the terms of agreement and paid subscription plans with Clipart.com and Fotolia.com.

Disclaimer

IMPORTANT: All information in this book is for news matter and entertainment purposes only and is not intended to be used in any direct or indirect violation of local, state, federal or international law(s). Any use of information and recommendations provided by this book is to be used at a visitor's sole discretion. The author, owner and publisher are not liable for any losses or damages incurred directly or indirectly.

Andrea was a tough girl in the comics.

Yes,and she has the scars to prove it.

Dale's time of death on the show was the same in the comic.

No, he died much earlier in the show.

Merle was not in the comic.

Yes, producers added him in the show.

Daryl was in the comic.

No, he was added in the show.

Hershel lied about his zombie farm in the comic.

No, he told the truth.

The Dixon brothers were part of the comic.

No, in the comic they did not exist at all.

the Latino Gang in the hospital did not exist in the comic.

Yes, they were added in the show.

In the Comic Shane was the main character.

No, it was Rick

Lori and Shane's affair was a one night stand in the comic.

Yes, in the comic it is shown in a flashback.

In the comic the Governor and his gang was the first organized group of survivors they encountered.

No, the prisoners were the first.

In the series, Lori and Shane's affair was prolonged compared to the comic.

Yes, in the comic it was only a one night stand.

In the comic, it was Lori who left Rick in the hospital and not Shane.

Yes, the hospital was not yet overrun by zombies.

In the comic, the Governor was a woman.

No, he was a man.

In the series, Hershel was a religious father figure.

Yes, the same in the comic.

In the comic, Otis was killed by zombies.

Yes, in the show he was sacrificed by Shane.

In the comic, Hershel had 2 kids, just like in the show.

No, in the comics he had 6 children.

Sophia becoming a zombie never happened in the comic.

Yes, she was safe at the farm.

In the comic, Daryl was killed by zombies.

No, he never existed in the comic.

In the Comic, Rick killed the human Shane and Carl killed the zombie Shane.

No, it was the other way around.

Andrea and Dale had a relationship in the comic.

Yes, Dale died early in the show.

The survivors were forced to flee the farm in the comic, because of the zombies approaching.

No, they were kicked out by Hershel.

Andrea was never separated from the group in the comic.

Yes, she always stayed with them.

Michonne was more sensitive in the comic.

Yes, she even had a relationship with Tyreese.

Shane was killed the same way in the show and in the comic.

Yes, he was shot.

Shane was killed the second time as a zombie, in both the show and the comic.

Yes, but by different characters.

In the comic Carl was actually a girl named Carla.

No, he was still Carl.

Rick was a soldier in the comic and not a policeman.

No, he was still a policeman .

Shane was Rick's Prisoner in the comic.

No, he was his partner.

In the comic the Governor was called the Mayor.

No, it was still the Governor.

Rick woke up in the hospital in both the comic and the show.

Yes, he was in a coma.

The word zombies was never mentioned in the show.

Yes, they were called walkers in the show.

The Governor call the zombies walkers.

No he called them biters.

There was no scene showing Morgan's wife in the comic.

Yes, it was added in the show to add drama.

In the comic they went back to the city to get Merle.

No, Merle did not exist in the comic.

Otis was fat in the comic and the show.

No, Otis was not fat in the comic.

The zombie barn was opened by accident in the comic.

Yes, the zombies escaped after.

Michonne held a spear in the comic.

No, she held a sword.

Daryl's weapon was a gun in the comic not a crossbow.

No, he did not exist in the comic.

Rick rode a motorcycle into the city.

No, he rode a horse.

The city Rick rode into was Atlanta.

Yes, he came in a horse.

In the Comic they did not stay in the barn for long.

Yes, they left sooner in the comic.

It was Ottis who shot Carl in both the comic and the TV series.

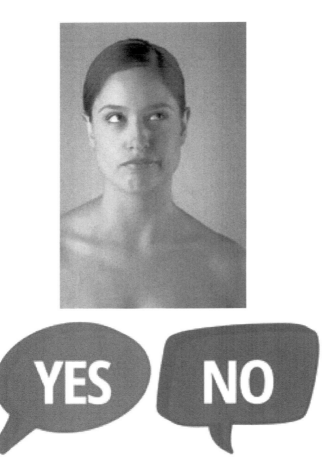

Yes, it was by accident.

In the comic Rick's group had a tank.

No, they did not.

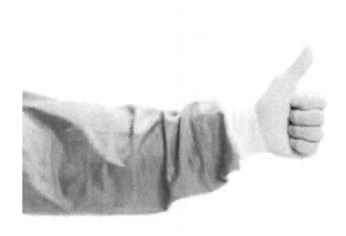

In the comic there was no CDC.

Yes, The CDC was added in the series.

Andrea had a baby with Dale in the comic.

No,They had a relationship but not a baby.

The governor is more hairy in the comic.

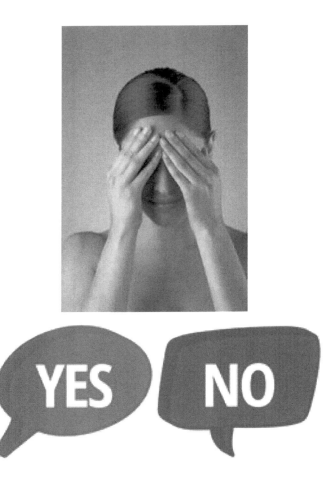

Yes, he has a clean cut in the series.

Rick always carries a crossbow in the series.

No, a pistol.

In the comic, zombies only bite at night.

No, they also bite during the day.

In the comic Rick is stressed out but he does not hallucinate as in the show.

Yes, in the comic he does not see dead people.

In the comic the Governor raped Michonne.

Yes, and he made Glenn Listen.

Michonne tortured the Governor in the comic.

Yes, as revenge.

21467678R00121

Made in the USA
Middletown, DE
30 June 2015